# You CAN Buy Word of Mouth!

### Long Term, Radio is Still the Cheapest Way to Persuade People to Become Your Customers

by

S. Randall Allsbury

S. Randall Allsbury

**You CAN Buy Word of Mouth!**
Long Term, Radio is Still the Cheapest
Way to Persuade People to Become
Your Customers

Copyright © 2013  S. Randall Allsbury

ISBN-13: 978-0615489346
(Allsbury Marketing, LLC.)

ISBN-10: 0615489346

## DEDICATION

This book is dedicated to you, the small business owner who risks it all to make this great country keep moving forward. Everything happening in this country is doing so because of entrepreneurs risking their money to create jobs and pay taxes. Churches, schools and all things government exist only because you are doing business.

Thank you for all you do!

# Table of Contents

## Read This First!

**I DO NOT WORK FOR ANY RADIO STATION. I DO NOT OWN A RADIO STATION. I DO NOT OWN STOCK IN ANY RADIO GROUP. I SIMPLY USE RADIO AS LARGE "WORD OF MOUTH" FOR MY CLIENTS.**

**I am sharing the individual parts of a recipe** with you. If you choose some parts of the recipe and leave out others, this may and probably will be a waste of your money.

The four main ingredients to using radio as your persuasive sales tool are:

1. Consistency (52 weeks a year for as long as you plan to stay in business)
2. Frequency (Multiple impressions a week, because sleep erases advertising messages.)
3. Meaningful Messages (Messages that are more about the interest of the customer and less about the interest of the business owner.)
4. Sharpen and repair the three areas of marketing. (See: The Marketing Boat)
    a. Business decisions in the Executive's office
    b. The A.C.E. (Actual Customer Experience)
    c. Outside your walls: Referrals, Reputation & Advertising

# INTRODUCTION

## What's good for the goose could KILL the gander!

What's good for big business in America is not necessarily so for small business America. Most small businesses advertising in America follow the lead of Nike, Coca-Cola and the biggest furniture store in their hometown. They set aside some advertising money and then divide it up between yellow pages, a website, the local newspaper, some seasonal radio ads and a three week TV campaign right before Christmas, not to mention the big sign at the right field fence at the high school baseball field.

## Does that sound like you?

You can't beat Goliath using his weapons. Little David went to the brook and picked up five stones. He focused all of his energy and resources in one direction with one stone. David didn't get a bag of rocks and throw them in all directions hoping one would land in the right place. He had a specific message aimed at a specific target. I believe David would have directed the next four stones at the exact same spot on the giant's forehead.

The weapon of big business is a huge advertising budget. They can afford to dominate every media outlet in your city. They don't need to have a strategy or compelling ads. The only thing they need for "gray-matter-real-estate" in the head of every person is a bunch of money. ***When you don't have a lot of money, you must have a better message and arrow shaped strategy.***

**For your small business… Radio can be the best choice, if you use it the right way. THE RIGHT WAY IS DIFFERENT THAN THE WAY 95% OF THE ADVERTISERS ARE USING IT.**

First, it can be used effectively no matter what size your budget. (From $500.00 a month to $25,000.00 a month.)

Hour by hour, radio has a fairly consistent audience and a very good ratings delivery system to find out how many people listen to each station in each market. With digital recording technology all you need is the ability to read and the right message.

*"Words start wars and end them, create love and choke it, bring us to laughter and joy and tears. Words cause men and women to willingly risk their lives, their fortunes and their sacred honor. Our world, as we know it, revolves on the power of words." - Roy H. Williams*

**Again, why radio?** Because it is a vehicle to deliver **your** words **intrusively** through people's *un-closable* ears.

# Chapter 1
# THE ADVANTAGES OF RADIO NO ONE EVER TALKS ABOUT

## Intrusive vs. Passive Media

I want to make my point very simply. Let's pretend your entire potential customer base could fit into one big school classroom.

One hundred chairs and one hundred people of all ages are doing life together.

Along one wall are various magazines appealing to different interests. There is a table in the corner with several copies of your city's daily newspaper. In another corner is a telephone resting on two different yellow pages directories. Every person in the room has either a computer, or a smart phone with Internet access. At the front of the room toward the ceiling is a speaker with music playing.

Throughout the day a few of the people read their magazine of choice. About 25% read the daily newspaper. Four of them walk over to the yellow pages, flip through and make a few phone calls. At one time or another all of them check their FaceBook pages and E-mail.

Your job is to reach these people through advertising. You have a dozen specific things you need to communicate to these people. You would like to communicate to all of them.

Would you try to target "your customer" through the magazine you think they read? Would you place an ad in your local newspaper? Would you buy a giant listing in a yellow pages directory? How about Google ads? Maybe an E-mail newsletter? What about an ad on FaceBook and a FaceBook page?

What if you could talk to them over the loud-speaker one time every hour?

**Passive Media** only works when the audience does something active. They have to read something on purpose. Did you know the only people who will notice your print ad, are the ones in the market for it today or happen to have a special interest in your product or service. Your print or written ad is invisible to everyone else.

It is very difficult to build a consistent audience through the written word. Great bloggers can build an audience of people who read their ramblings every week. A few can build an E-Newsletter people will read every week.

**Intrusive Media** goes right into people's un-closable ears. Getting people to pay attention and remember what they heard is up to you. If you begin by saying something more interesting than what they are thinking right now, you gain their attention. If you continue to educate and entertain, you keep their attention. If you do this consistently and frequently, you can use words to persuade them to become your customers and/or tell others about your products and services.

*I am not saying* all people listen to commercial radio. That would be silly. I am saying there are tens of thousands and most likely hundreds of thousands of people listening to commercial radio in your hometown.

*You can speak to them and develop a relationship with them over time, by speaking to them in their language about what matters to them.*

I am also not saying, "Passive Media does not work". *I am simply saying it is easier to reach an audience consistently and frequently through intrusive media*, taking advantage of *listener pattern predictability.*

**More things no one talks about…**

•*Echoic Intrusiveness*---You can close your eyes, but you cannot close your ears. You continue to hear even when you look away. If your radio is on, the sound is going in your ears. When you are fast asleep you can hear people talking and hear things that go "bump!" in the night.

•*Echoic Retention*---Any competent cognitive neuroscientist will confirm that echoic memory (audio) is vastly superior to iconic memory (visual). Words, statements, phrases, jingles, and songs, which surprise Broca's Area of the brain, are much more easily implanted and recalled than visual images. (Broca's Area is the gatekeeper of the brain. When you hear cliché, boring and predictable ads, the gate closes and the message is ignored.)

•*Involuntary Echoic Retention*---Causes people to remember things they never committed to memory, and a working knowledge of it gives one the ability to work miracles through the power of words. Echoic retention and the power of words is the heart and soul of advertising, though very few ad professionals understand it.

•*Neural Personalization of the Message*---Great writers understand that the word "You" conjures up a different mental image in every human mind. One of the greatest advantages of radio is the absence of visual images. This allows the radio ad to be about the listener, personally.

•*Listener Pattern Predictability*---It is easier to achieve weekly frequency with the same listener on the radio than it is to repeatedly find the same viewer on television or the same reader in a print ad. Consequently, it's much easier to win the battle of Frequency vs. Sleep (ad memory fades with sleep) using radio.

**Chapter 2**

**MAKING CENTS WITH RADIO**

The only way you can persuade people to become your customer is over time. This is the beauty of *Listener Pattern Predictability.* Done right, you can educate and win new customers over time by feeding them a little bit of information at a time.

No single commercial can transfer enough information for branding to take place, but a series of ads in a long campaign can. I look at it this way: Your business, life and values is an entire book of information. Each ad of your long-term campaign is a chapter of this book. I will go into more detail when I talk about copy writing.

WHY IS BRANDING LONG TERM ON THE RADIO THE BEST BUY IN MEDIA?

Next, I am going to show you a one week snapshot of a real branding schedule I bought a few years ago.

## Actual Schedule:

| | Daypart | Weeks | Spot Length | SPOTS | RATE | TOTAL COST | FREQ | AVERAGE PERSONS | NET REACH |
|---|---|---|---|---|---|---|---|---|---|
| 1 | M-F 6A-12N | 1 | :60 | 13 | $75 | $975.00 | 3.1 | 12,000 | 51,100 |
| 2 | Kxxx -FM | 1 | | 13 | $75 | $975.00 | 3.1 | 12,000 | 51,100 |
| 3 | TOTALS: | 1 | | 13 | $75 | $975.00 | 3.1 | 12,000 | 51,100 |

When ads will run.

Radio Station

How many per wk.

Dollars per ad

Cost per week

Reach and Frequency is how many times, how many people will hear your ad each week….

**Radio: Making cents out of radio...**

•13 ads X's $75 = $975 per week

•$975 X's 52 weeks = $50,700

•52 weeks X's 3 frequency = 156 times

•$50,700 divided by 51,100 listeners = 99.2 cents per listener annually

•<u>You are paying 99.2 cents to reach the average listener 3 times a week for 52 weeks!!!</u>

*If you have little or no ad budget, $975.00 a week is way too much to start with. Next, are numbers from a smaller station. You will notice you are reaching 20,800 people a week instead of 51,100. Notice though, that the cost per listener dropped from 99.2 cents to 53 cents per listener.* ***I have purchased 52 week branding schedules for as little as $150.00 per week, reaching 5000 people a week.***

Radio: Making cents out of radio... <u>Smaller Station</u>

•20 ads X's $20 = $400 per week

•$400 X's 52 weeks = $20,800

•52 weeks X's 3 frequency = 156 times

•$20,800 divided by 39,800 listeners = 53 cents per listener annually

•<u>You are paying 53 cents to reach the average listener 3 times a week for 52 weeks!!!</u>

Actual Schedule: **Smaller Station**

| | Daypart | Weeks | Spot Length | SPOTS | RATE | TOTAL COST | FREQ | AVERAGE PERSONS | NET REACH |
|---|---|---|---|---|---|---|---|---|---|
| 1 | M-F 6A-12N | 1 | :60 | 20 | $20 | $400.00 | 3.0 | 1800 | 20,800 |
| 2 | Kxxx - AM | 1 | | 20 | $20 | $400.00 | 3.0 | 1800 | 20,800 |
| 3 | TOTALS: | 1 | | 20 | $20 | $400.00 | 3.0 | 1800 | 20,800 |

When ads will run.

Radio Station

How many per wk.

Dollars per ad

Cost per week

Reach and Frequency is how many times, how many people will hear your ad each week….

Chapter **3**

**THE EARS HAVE IT!**

When my wife was in college, her psychology professor
challenged the class to do something out of their
comfort zone. He handed out a list of possibilities, and
from that list she chose a police ride-along. She rode
around in a squad car on a Friday night from midnight to
6:00am. At one point they were following a possible
stolen car. The man in front of them turned, slammed on
his breaks, got out, looked directly at them and ran down
a dark alley. The officer took chase and my wife stayed
in the cruiser. The officer came back empty handed,
looked at my wife and asked, "Wouldn't you describe
him as a tall slim black man with a red bandana on his
head?" "Actually," she said, "I thought he was a white
guy with an orange base-ball cap." I don't remember his
exact description when they caught him, but I do recall
neither of them was right.

Most advertisers who have a product to sell almost
always think people need to *see* what they are buying.

Most of the time however, what they are purchasing is not really what they are *buying*. When most people buy a Hummer SUV, they are not buying it because they need a three ton vehicle to get to the office. They are buying it to look down into the cars next to them at stop lights. They are making a statement in today's society. They may even be trying to make up for certain physical deficiencies. You don't need pictures of what you are buying, you need the power of words describing the benefits of owning the product.

I have a large family, when traveling in the car on vacation I generally handle the adventures inside the car pretty well. That is, until we get into traffic in an unfamiliar city. I immediately ask everyone to play "the quiet game". Why? Because I can't close my ears and the possible verbal distraction could prove to be very unsafe for the travelers. Have you ever stopped to think about it? You can close your eyes, but you cannot close your ears. Sound is all encompassing. It is enticing and alluring. You hear and retain information even when you're not listening. You hear even when you're fast asleep. How else would your alarm clock wake you in the morning?

One of the greatest myths in the world today is that "we remember more of what we see than what we hear." In fact, quite the opposite is true. The great scientist of the eye, Josef Albers, says it in chapter one of his landmark book, *Interaction of Color*: "The visual memory is very poor in comparison with our auditory memory."

God's primary gift to you, me, and the rest of the human race is our ability to attach meanings to sounds. This is accomplished in three highly specialized parts of your brain--Broca's area, Wernicke's area and the Auditory Association area. In fact, your physical ability to coordinate the movements of your diaphragm, larynx, tongue, and lips so that you can produce human speech is also owed to Broca's Area, a specialized extension of Auditory Association into the Motor Association cortex.

I have been challenged by dyslexia most of my life. I was married for twelve years when my wife began pointing it out to me. It is very easy for me to stare at words and not read a thing unless I really concentrate. The written word has no meaning until the brain has translated it into the spoken word it represents. I'm sure you've been there when you are tired. You're reading a book and suddenly realize you've read the same paragraph four times and have no idea what it says. Yes, your eyes were sending the written symbols to your brain, but those symbols were no longer being translated into the sounds they represent. According to neurologists, it takes the average reader approximately 28 percent longer to understand the written word than to understand the same word when spoken. This is because the written word must be translated into the spoken word before it can be understood.

**Why radio?**

Because the human brain is wired for sound, in advertising we might as well take advantage of God's creation.

**Chapter 4**

**RADIO'S REMOTE BROADCAST**

Broadcasting a radio show from your location is a favorite of both radio sales reps and business owners. Both get their instant gratification *itches* scratched. The sales rep makes a decent one-time sale and gets to see the "power" of his or her radio station as it drives traffic to a given location.

**THE EFFECTIVENESS OF A REMOTE BROADCAST IS ALSO DEPENDENT ON THE MESSAGE OR CENTRAL THEME OF THE EVENT. <u>DOES ANYONE CARE ABOUT WHAT WE ARE SELLING?</u>**

In a world of advertising insecurity the business owner gets some direct response for the dollars he spends.

As much as remotes make business people feel good about the store traffic, a broadcast from your location *should* be used to make the radio listeners feel good about your business. Why? Because there are about 200 times more people listening to the radio than will show up to your event. Pay your radio host or DJ a few extra bucks to describe your store in detail every chance they get. Have them describe the feeling people will get when they walk into your store. They should mention your salespeople by name and describe them on air.

To help you understand what to say on the air, think about people in their homes and cars listening to the radio. Remember people are interested in what matters to them. Write up a list of benefits of shopping at your location, purchasing your products and services. Stay away from describing what matters to you the business owner, instead ask your radio host or DJ help describe what would matter to people in the real world. As they talk, have them share the details. Not like in a commercial, but as a recommendation from a friend. People enjoy buying from friends; people hate being *sold to* by strangers.

You can actually begin a relationship with the listener through the DJ and radio host.

Remember this: *"All things being equal, people will do business with people they like. All things not being equal, people will do business with people they like."*

If you really must, go ahead and let the station bring out the big banners, the dunk tank, and the free hot dogs. Will that really make people feel better about you and think of you first when they need your product or service?

**Chapter 5**

**TALK RADIO**

Listeners to these stations are actually listening and hearing what is being said. Their ears are still tuned in to the radio even during commercial breaks. It's not just background music. Talk radio is program driven instead of day-part driven like music radio. Which means it's more like TV without the picture. People tune in to specific shows at specific times of day.

When advertising, instead of buying a wide schedule from 6:00AM to 7:00PM, you're better off buying your ads during a specific show. The city I live in, airs Glenn Beck, the Rush Limbaugh Show and Sean Hannity, Monday through Friday from 8:00am to 5:00PM. Glen is on from 8:00am to 11:00am, Rush is on from 11:00am to 2:00pm and Hannity is on from 2:00pm to 5:00pm. There's no bigger single audience on any radio stations anywhere in the city. You can buy fifteen ads a week, one per hour during the Rush Limbaugh Show and reach more people than many radio stations reach 24 hours a day, seven days a week. Each area of the country is different; in some cities the Dave Ramsey Show is huge, in others it's Sean Hannity or even Bill O'Reilly. You can find out from your talk radio sales rep what shows have the most listeners or what shows have an audience you can afford with your budget.

Chapter **6**

**SPEED UP PEOPLE LIKING YOU…**

This can happen by having someone people already like
speaking on your behalf. Most talk radio stations have at
least one local talk show host. If the talk show host likes
what you do, he or she can be persuaded to do live
endorsements for your business. (If the price is right.)
Before, during or after a commercial break the host can
do a live commercial for your business.  It is always best
when they actually use your product or service. The live
ad should be written more like a recommendation than a
commercial. I call it *big* " word of mouth" advertising.

I'll always remember what one of my first sales
managers, Mike Beckner told me:  ***"Facts tell, stories
sell"***. Facts give you the information and stories bring in
the emotion. People make decisions emotionally and
then back them up intellectually.  The talk show host
must tell his own story about his experience with your
product or service. The owner of the business should
develop a relationship with the host.  You want the host

to talk about you as a friend. *After all, there's nothing quite as believable as the truth*.

THE DOWN SIDE TO HAVING SOMEONE ELSE PITCH YOUR PRODUCTS AND SERVICES IS EVENTUALLY THEY QUIT, MOVE AWAY OR DIE.

Chapter **7**

**BLOCK TIME**

Infomercials and brokered shows are another advantage of talk radio. This is the ability to buy blocks of airtime on radio. With a matter of a few phone calls and a few appointments you can hire a radio host and a production professional to assist you in creating your own radio infomercial. The cost will vary from one market to another. In some cases unions may have something to do with fee schedules. You can hire the radio host and a production director and rent studio time to record your infomercial. You simply have the host ask you a predetermined group of questions about the benefits of doing business with your company. Don't try to reinvent the wheel. Listen to other infomercials on your local stations and simply copy what they're doing. Almost any radio production director can edit your infomercial to be twenty-two, twenty-four or twenty-eight minutes in length. This depending on what the radio station needs in half-hour segments. In some cases the news eats up several minutes of your half hour. (Keep that in mind when you are negotiating your rate for the half hour segment.) You can write and produce several shows, then rotate them every week. Everything you write and produce must sound like a real show. It must be entertaining and educational. Remember if it sounds like a commercial it's a *bad infomercial*.

Chapter **8**

## LIVE BROKERED SHOWS

If you have the talent, the time, and the ability to pull it off, some radio stations will allow you to purchase your own radio show. This is a big undertaking.

You have to be willing to commit to showing up to the studio every week, as long as the contract states. You must also study and prepare for every show. Count on preparing two or three hours minimum for every hour you're on the air. Professional radio hosts work very hard to make what they do sound easy. Many new radio hosts get started thinking callers will help them carry the show. They think people will start calling in no matter what the topic. It takes time, practice, and skill to say things in an engaging way getting people to call in and talk. In the beginning you better be prepared for it to be you and the listeners, you talking and them listening. Less than one percent of listeners will ever call in on any radio show.

The advantage of actually being on the radio every week live and in person is that over time you become the expert in your field to that station's listeners if you work hard and come across as a professional. The beauty of a weekly live talk show is that people have the ability to actually call you and get information and answers to their problems directly from you. Most of the time the callers will be asking questions hundreds of other listeners also want to hear. If you do begin your own radio show, give yourself at least a year to get the hang of it. You'll make people feel the best about you and when they are in need of your product or service, they'll think of you first.

People who get really good hosting their own brokered show begin developing an audience. In some cases they can sell commercials during their show to third parties and subsidize their own advertising costs.

**Chapter 9**

## THERE ARE ONLY TWO KINDS OF ADVERTISING...

1.  **You are telling people about an event you want them to participate in right now.**

    Any time you put a price and an item in an ad and mention the word SALE, you have advertised an event. The only people who notice or really hear your event/sale ad are the people who are in the market today for your product or service. That only about 2% of the population, no matter what your business.

    Most business owners who step out into the advertising world only dabble in event advertising. Sadly, they only reach the 2% and their ad remains invisible to the other 98%.

    If you are promoting an event, you need lots of repetition. Reminder after reminder about your event. There is a deadline and you need an urgent message and description.

2. **You are trying to persuade people to become your long-term customers. I call this real BRANDING.**

BRANDING is advertising to the same crowd long term and persuading them to like you and feel best about you over time. "People do business with people they like!"

When you have done it right, people will call you first WHEN they come in need of your product or service.

If you are smart, you have a product or service that everyone needs eventually. Hopefully you have something everyone needs multiple times a year.

**Chapter 10**

**COMMUNICATING IN AN**

**OVER-COMMUNICATED WORLD**

We are bombarded by thousands of commercial messages every day. Driving in our cars we see and read all kinds of billboards, business marquees, and bumper stickers. We turn on our radios, our TV sets, we even hear ads over the telephone when we are put on hold. They're on key chains, pens, pencils, plastered all over the event arenas, on Web sites, FaceBook, calendars, elevators, and even in bathroom stalls. If people see it or hear it, someone will try to sell it as advertising space.

**Positioning**

Jack Trout and Al Ries came up with these terms decades ago. They are still true. We humans only remember an average of three choices for any business product category. If you don't believe this, test it for yourself. Do a few informal surveys. Choose about five different products or services and ask people in your world to name as many brands as they can. You'll find on average they can name about 3 for each. Picture a ladder in the mind of each potential customer. We call it "the positioning ladder". If your business is not on one of the top three rungs of the ladder, you'll never be considered. Are you doing anything pro-active to get on anyone's top three rungs? How much advertising will get you there?

**Chapter 11**

**FIVE LEVELS OF COMMUNICATION**

As I talk to business owners, I continually ask them to step out of their reality and join me in the reality the rest of us are experiencing.  Many business owners would like to believe if every person in town heard about them one time, they would call *them* for their products or services.

In reality, there are five levels of communication and we must bring potential customers through all five.

1. Unawareness

2. Awareness

3. Comprehension

4. Conviction

5. Action

You might be saying, "Wait a minute, I ran an ad only one time and got results." You reached people who needed your product or service so bad they called you immediately. Depending on how well you served them, you may or may not now be on their positioning ladder.

When advertising to the masses, it takes time to get up the steps of the ladders in their minds. Reaching one of the top three rungs takes time. Advertising the right way is not an event; it's an ongoing process.

Chapter **12**

## REACHING THE "RIGHT" PEOPLE

It's time for you to stop trying to reach the "right" people and begin reaching someone effectively. Stop looking at people as though they are divided into hard groups who never talk to one another. On average, everyone has a circle of influence of approximately 200 people. Which means the average person has about 200 friends and acquaintances. When we are deeply touched by something (whether good or bad), we tell people in our circle. If you buy a new appliance, receive excellent service, and you're very happy with the product, you tell people. If it breaks the first time you use it, you *really* tell people.

### 1 – 11 – 55

At a leadership conference a few years back, I heard John Maxwell talk about the 1-11-55 principle. He said customers who have a bad experience with your business, on average will tell eleven people. Those eleven will tell about five more people. If people have a bad experience with you or your business, almost fifty-five people will find out about it. If people have an "average" or "expected" experience with your business, they really don't tell anyone. They got what they expected. If they have an outstanding, incredible, best-service-ever experience with you, they will tell an average of six people, who will tell four (if you are lucky). Twenty-four people might hear about your great service.

Is this hard to believe? When you buy a new car and everything works great, what do you do? You drive it! If you get in your new car and the slightest thing is wrong, what do you do? You squeal to anyone who will listen.

**Get the Right Word Out**

Stop trying to reach the *right* person. Instead, reach someone with a message that will make *them* feel best about *you*. When they come in need of your product or service, they will call you first.

Chapter 13

## THE GOOSE AND THE GANDER (MEDIA MIX)

Media Mix is simply trying to buy two or more media outlets with your dollars. Unless you have the budget of Nike or Coca-Cola, media mix is a media mess. Mistakenly, business owners think if they buy a little TV and a little radio and a little newspaper and one billboard, the combination will reach a large group of people. There is a lot of noise out there. If you want to get into people's long-term chemical memory, your message and delivery vehicle *must be focused.*

Picture your message as the point on the nose of a Rhinoceros. Make your media choice and drive all four thousand pounds of your message into the minds of the audience.

If you dilute your message over several different media outlets, no one will see or hear any of your ads enough to make it through the five levels of communication.

## 100,000 people once, or 10,000 people ten times?

You are at the Super Bowl. The Superdome is packed with 100,000 plus cheering fans. The man in charge gives you the opportunity to talk to the people in the stadium about your business. He offers you two choices; you can get on the intercom and talk to the entire crowd one time for sixty seconds or they will section off one tenth of the stadium and he will let you talk to *them* ten times during the game, 60 seconds each time. Which would you choose? We live in an over communicated society; I hope you would choose the latter!

**Chapter 14**
**DOES SIZE MATTER?**

Advertising sales reps all want to have the biggest listening audience. "We have the most listeners age 25 to 54" or "We have the largest audience age 12 plus". It *is* important to reach as many people as you can afford. Do you have to advertise on the biggest station in town to get results?

**The right message, consistently and frequently delivered** works when you are reaching 5,000 people or 100,000 people. You obviously pay less to reach 5,000 people. At one point in my radio ad selling career I sold for one station that had 120,000 listeners a week and another having about 25,000 per week. On the bigger station, the Monday through Friday daytime ads averaged about $125 for one sixty second commercial. On the smaller station the same ad cost $25.

When I had a good message and enough ads running every week, my clients had very nice results. The most dramatic growth came from the smaller station. A heat and air company advertising on the smaller station went from $70,000 per month in gross sales to over $200,000 per month in gross sales in the first year. They ran twenty-five ads per week Monday through Friday from 6:00am to 7:00pm every week. Every time I stopped by for a visit, the owner let me know 8 out of 10 referrals came from the radio.

The right message for this client was written by me and voiced by Dave Ramsey on the smaller local talk radio station his show was on. *After Dave Ramsey's staff did a background check* on my client, the client only had to pay $250 for his three month endorsement. That was a decade ago. Today Dave's empire and audience is much bigger. He currently charges $1000 every three months or $4000 annually per individual market.

Any time you can get someone people like and trust to voice your ads, you are way ahead.

**"All things being equal, people do business with people they like. All things not being equal, people do business with people they like!"**

**Chapter 15**

**YOU NEED SOMEONE YOU DON'T KNOW TO INTRODUCE YOU TO YOURSELF**

Business owners are uniquely unqualified to tell people about their business or to write their own commercials. Why? It's like asking a fish to describe water. They are so engulfed in what they do in their world, they no longer see themselves as real.

Zig Zigler tells about purchasing a drill bit. No one really needs a one-quarter inch drill bit. What they need is a one-quarter inch hole. Never describe the drill bit itself, describe what it will do for them.

My wife and I have lost some weight this past year. I was never really interested in buying scales until I started losing weight. I really could care less how my bathroom scales work, what type of battery it uses or computer chip. I simply want to know how much I weigh.

I have an acquaintance that wanted to buy a home computer years ago. He didn't know anything about computers. He went to a local computer store owned and operated by a computer nerd. My friend walked in and said, "I want to buy a computer." The business owner asked, "How much RAM do you need?" His next question was, "How much hard drive space will you need?" My friend immediately realized he was totally unqualified to buy a computer. His eyes glazed over and he walked out. A few days later he stopped by another computer store to begin his research to become qualified to buy a computer. A teenager was stocking shelves and asked him why he was buying a computer. "Well, I want to play some games with my son and my wife heard about a recipe program she would like to use. I have also been thinking about balancing my checkbook with a computer program." The teenager pointed across the room at one of the smaller computer and said, "This one will do everything you want and a lot more. It should last for a few years." The young man pointed out a few other programs the family would enjoy. My friend dropped some serious coin that day because someone was willing and able to speak his language.

Many times business owners need someone else to point out why people "really" do business with them.

## Chapter 16
## COPYWRITNG FOR RADIO

**Basically, if it sounds like a commercial, it's a bad commercial.**

Most ads written today are crammed full of who, what, when and where.  They leave out the most important question of all: "why".

I don't care *who, what, when or where* until you first convince me of *why*. Most advertising sounds like one of my kids when they were toddlers. "Me, me, me… look at me… watch me!"  Poor advertising is about the business, rich advertising is about the listener.

**STAY AWAY FROM ALL "AD-SPEAK"** it's Invisible.

**People ignore it and are tired of it!**

**George Carlin has a comedy bit called "Advertising Lullaby". It is the best list of Ad-Speak ever created.**

## GEORGE CARLIN AD SPEAK

Quality, value, style, service, selection, convenience
Economy, savings, performance, experience,
hospitality
Low rates, friendly service, <u>name brands</u>, easy
terms
Affordable prices, money-back guarantee.

Free installation, free admission, free appraisal, free
alterations,
Free delivery, free estimates, free home trial, and
free parking.

No cash? No problem! No kidding! No fuss, no
muss,
No risk, no obligation, no red tape, no down
payment,
No entry fee, no hidden charges, no purchase
necessary,
No one will call on you, no payments or interest till
September.

Limited time only, though, so act now, order today,
send no money,
Offer good while supplies last, two to a customer,
each item sold separately,
Batteries not included, mileage may vary, all sales
are final,
Allow six weeks for delivery, some items not

available,
Some assembly required, some restrictions may apply.

So come on in for a free demonstration and a free consultation
with our friendly, professional staff. Our experienced and
knowledgeable <u>sales representatives</u>

will help you make a
selection that's just right for you and just right for your budget.

And say, don't forget to pick up your free gift: a classic deluxe
custom designer luxury prestige high-quality premium select
gourmet pocket pencil sharpener.Yours for the asking,
no purchase necessary.It's our way of saying thank you.

And if you act now, we'll include an extra added free complimentary
bonus gift at no cost to you: a classic deluxe custom designer
luxury prestige high-quality premium select gourmet combination
key ring, magnifying glass, and garden hose, in a

genuine
imitation leather-style carrying case with authentic
vinyl trim.
Yours for the asking, no purchase necessary.

It's our way of
saying thank you.

The more ad-speak you cram in your commercials, the more invisible they become. They are nothing cliché. A cliché  is an over-used phrases no one believes.

## 10 Things to Avoid When Writing Ads

I have always been a believe that "Facts Tell and Stories Sell". I believe people make most all decisions emotionally.

You can make a pretty good argument about two doctors making a life or death decision over the "facts" presented to them in a diagnosis. At the end of the day, they/you are forced to trust "facts". *You have to have faith in the facts, making it an emotional decision.*

**My job is to sell stuff for people using media. To do it well, I have to tell stories. I decided to become a better story teller, by studying the best in the country. I bought the book STORY, by Robert McKee. He is the number one go to guy regarding movie screenplays in the country. I found a YouTube video of Mr. McKee called *10 Problems To Avoid With Dialogue In Screenplays.* Wow, these are pretty much the same things I try to avoid when writing commercials that don't sound like commercials!**

I am calling this "10 Things to Avoid When Writing Ads"

1. Repetitiousness
   a. Make sure you don't say the same thing over and over and over using the same words.
2. Trightness
   a. Dialog filled with clichés
3. Character Neutral Language
   a. Using "all-purpose" lines that anyone could say in the same situation. Almost a

cliché, but more of a "Duhhh, that is obvious!"

4. Ostentation

    a. The writer using "flowery" with very artistic words to show their artsyness.

5. Arid Speech

    a. Dry, "Ivy-League" and Pretentious wording, trying to sound like an intellectual.

6. Over-Statement

    a. "Brawny" words with puny motivation. Often profanity is used when there is no substance.

7. Talking Wallpaper

    a. The humdrum chit-chat of "Hi, how are you? I am fine. The weather is fine." Writers add this stuff to sound natural, but no one really speaks this way.

8. Forced Exposition

    a. One character telling another character what they both already know, in order for the reader or audience to learn important facts of the story.

9. Malformation

   a. Scenes that are badly shaped. The audience
      or reader becomes distracted when their
      brain is screaming: "This is not a
      plausible situation."

10. Writing Dialog "On the Nose"

   a. Writing or saying exactly what the
      character is thinking and feeling without
      any sub-text. This is treating the audience
      or reader like they are stupid and
      insulting their intelligence with too many
      words.

If you fancy yourself a story-teller, a preacher,
teacher or public speaker, you might consider
avoiding these as well.

**Chapter 17**

**GOOD ADS VS. BAD ADS**

**Focus on the listener, not on the business.**

**Here are two examples for an attorney:**

**Business Focused---** *"At Johnson Law Firm, we have attorneys to deal with every legal challenge in the courts. Stacie Johnson specializes in divorce and custody cases. Brent Johnson is an expert in Elder Law including Wills, Trusts and Guardianships. Seth Wilson handles criminal law cases and Julia Fredrickson really knows how to get you your money if you are injured in an accident. The attorneys at Johnson Law Firm really care about you and your challenges. Call Johnson Law Firm today for a free consultation at 751-2323. That's 751-2323. You can also stop by the Johnson Law Firm at 1800 E. Memorial."*

**Now listen to the customer-focused ad for the same advertiser:**

**Listener Focused---** *"As a loving parent, there is only one thing of real value in your life, your children. You worry about them at school; you help them with homework and the everyday challenges they face. You've provided the loving nest they've enjoyed. As the tornado of divorce rocks your home, there are many things you are uncertain of. There is one thing in which you are very confident. Your children want to be with you and need to be with you. Stacie Johnson specializes in divorce and custody cases. She has been standing shoulder to shoulder next to people like you for the past seventeen years. Call Johnson Law Firm for a free consultation. JohnsonLaw.com"*

**Let's try it with a <u>dentist commercial:</u>**

**Business Focused---**"*This is Dr. Terry Miller of Miller Dentistry. I have been a dentist right here in metro for fifteen years. At Miller Dentistry we have an excellent staff of hygienists and assistants. They are all very friendly and caring. We do general dentistry as well as cosmetic dentistry. Call 555-1234 and ask about our current new-patient special. At Miller Dentistry you can get a cleaning, exam, x-*

*rays and teeth-whitening for only 199 dollars. This is a 500 dollar value. We honor most all dental insurance plans, we accept all major credit cards and have an excellent in-house payment plan. Our office is conveniently located at 5858 North West Expressway. Call ahead and make your appointment for your cleaning, exam, x-ray and teeth-whitening special. Remember it's only 199 dollars for a 500 dollar value. Call 555-1234"*

**Listener Focused---**"*Are you in sales? One expert said Selling is transferring confidence. A big part of transferring confidence is your smile. "People who don't smile, don't sell". Is there something preventing you from being confident? If you have a missing tooth, a broken one, or a dark colored tooth or a cavity right up front, it **can** be fixed. In most cases your teeth can look like new. You might only need to have your teeth whitened. Dr. Cox has a kit you can take home with you. You treat your teeth every day for up to two hours over a few weeks. You end up with a whiter, brighter and more confident smile. The best thing for you to do is to make an* *appointment for a simple check up to see if this system will work for you. You will love the staff at JimCoxDental.com. Call Becky or Ann today for your appointment. The number is 387-5858, that's 387-5858. People who have nice white teeth have more confidence and love to smile. Visit the website at JimCoxDental.com"*

**In my opinion this is important for you to see examples of different businesses.**

**Let's do this one more time for a furniture store:**

**Business Focused---** *"Come on down to Eddy's Furniture this Friday and Saturday. We are having our annual I.R.S. sale! Inventory Reduction Sale! At Eddy's furniture the 2011 models have arrived and the 2010 furniture must go. Our lack of space is your lucky day this Friday and Saturday. We are slashing prices to make room. Bedroom suites are 50% off. Mattresses are marked down 25%. Name brand sectionals and recliners are up to 50% off. We also have huge savings on TVs and entertainment* *centers. This I.R.S. sale is the perfect time for you to spend your tax refund check. There will never be another sale like this at Eddy's Furniture! It starts this Friday morning at 9am and ends Saturday night at 9pm. Eddy's Furniture is located at the west end of North Park Mall at the intersection of Reno and 122$^{nd}$ street. Don't Miss Out!"*

**Listener Focused---** *"Are you the last man on your block still watching your favorite team play on an old, bulky, analog TV set? Are you trying to watch Hi-Definition movies on a No-Definition screen? And when you are watching movies, you either have a black space at the top and bottom of your screen or both ends of the movie are cut off and you are missing part of every scene. There is no excuse for you to be suffering this way. You can now afford Champaign on your beer budget! You can afford to step into the HD TV world! The everyday price for a 26 inch LCD 1080p Flat-screen TV at Eddy's Furniture is 300 dollars. The everyday price for a 42 inch LCD 1080p Flat-screen TV is only 700 dollars! You will be proud to invite the guys over to watch* *the next game. See our selection online at EddysFurniture.com"*

The goal is to cause the customer to imagine himself or herself behind "the wheel", experiencing all the images we're describing.  We humans can only do what we first imagine ourselves doing.

Are you beginning to catch on?

The most important parts of a long term branding ad are the beginning and the ending. We call it the First Mental Image and the Last Mental Image. (The Primacy Effect and the Recency Effect.)

The beginning of the ad must entice your audience to "stay tuned". You must include clear mental images the listener can *see* and *feel*. At the end of your ad you must describe the action you would like them to take or the last image you want to leave with them .

## Chapter 18

## WRITING THE SHORT TERM AD

Most ads out there in media world are short-term ads. The biggest problem with short-term ads is they contain short-term information. Our brain erases information it no longer needs. Real branding never takes place and if your advertising is a series of short-term ads, you train the listener or reader to wait for the next sale event.

Chuck Mefford of Lighthouse Communications teaches an easy way to write an ad for an event, promotion or sale. He calls it U.T.O.P.I.A., which stands for:

Urgency---What is the time limit?

Theme---What is the event about?

Offer---What is the benefit to the customer? (Why Factor)

Price---What is the price?

Item---What are they buying?

Action---Call to action!

Include each of these in your ad and you will cover your bases.

Run your UTOPIA ad every hour on the radio for one to two weeks before your event.

## Chapter 19
## SCHEDULING YOUR COMMERCIALS

There are basically only two ways to schedule your ads. You are either promoting an event, or you're doing a long term branding campaign. Everything else is a mixture of the two.

### Short Term or Event Scheduling

It's 7:00AM and I am walking out the door headed to the office. As I'm leaving my wife asks me to bring home milk and bread when I come home from work. At that point, the odds of me remembering are about 25 percent. If she calls me at noon and reminds me, the chances jump to about 50 percent. If she sends me an e-mail mid-afternoon, we are up to about 75 percent. If she calls me on my cell phone as I'm leaving the office, she just hit 100 percent and I'm bringing home milk and bread. (This is not a true illustration; my wife would have to remind me at least ten times for me to remember.)

When you are planning an event like a concert or a big sale, you have plenty of time to think about it, process it, and plan it in your mind. You are excited about it and expect everyone else to be as well. Let me remind you, there are five levels of communication, unawareness, awareness, comprehension, conviction, and action.

The listener must hear your message at least five times to have a good impact. You must also keep in mind your message is only going to be "really" heard by people who already have an interest in what you are selling or planning. People are either interested, or they are not. The best way to schedule your ads for an event is to run one ad per hour every hour. Plan your schedule backwards until you run out of money. Which means you run an ad one hour before your event, one ad two hours before your event, one ad three hours before your event and so on. Buy one ad per hour for as many days as possible leading up to your event from 6 AM to 7 PM. If you have the budget, do it for twelve days prior to your event. If you still have money left over, go back and fill in the overnight hours. (7:00pm to 6:00am)

*Again this is about reminding the listeners over and over and over about your event.*

**Branding Scheduling**

Once you begin a branding campaign, never, ever stop unless you plan on closing your business for good. It only works better as time goes on. Run your schedule fifty-two weeks per year.

**Branding is about making people feel best about you over time.** When they are in need of your product or service, they will think of you first. Hopefully your message has made them feel best about you.

You want a minimum frequency of *three* every week. (I prefer 4-5.)

**Frequency** *is radio lingo for how many times the average listener hears your ad.* Over many years of scheduling we have discovered an average. Buying about 20-25 ads per week, Monday through Friday, 6:00AM to 7:00PM, you'll end up with about a three frequency. If you can't afford 6:00AM to 7:00PM, buy the same frequency from 7:00PM to midnight or from midnight to 6:00AM. Overnight schedules are wonderfully under-priced. Yes, there are people listening to the radio at 3 AM. There are not as many, but you're only going to be paying a few bucks for each ad.

Do I need to remind you, *your message matters*?

**Avoid Wide Rotators**

A wide rotator is an ad scheduled from 6:00am to midnight or midnight to midnight. This ad may run morning, noon, evening, or night. Yes, you'll be given a low rate on the wide rotator, but you'll have a difficult time getting enough frequency with any listener. Make sure your ads are scheduled in the same day-part every week. A good schedule might be running twelve ads per week, Monday through Friday, 6:00am to 10:00am, reaching 75,000 people each week. If you can't afford daytime rates, you might buy twenty ads per week, Monday through Friday, 7:00pm to midnight reaching 18,000 people per week. It's better to achieve "Top of Mind

Awareness" with 18,000 people, than no awareness with 1,000,000 people!

**Chapter 20**

**WHAT IS BRANDING, REALLY?**

In chapter eight I introduced you to an effective branding schedule. Let's go into more detail about what branding really is. At Wizard Academy (www.wizardacademy.com) south of Austin Texas, Roy H. Williams teaches that Ivan Pavlov discovered true branding, for which he won a Nobel Prize in 1904. He goes on to say branding is the implementation of an associative memory in combination with a recall cue.

**An Associative Memory**

If I say: "Great Taste, Less Filling". You think of Miller Light.

If I say: "Like a Good Neighbor…" You think of State Farm Insurance.

If I say: "We'll leave the light on for you." You think of Motel 6.

In your mind, one memory has been linked to another memory. A recall cue is a mental trigger, which prompts the listener to take a prescribed action at an appointed time. There are three keys to implementing an associative memory in the mind of the customer.

## Key Number One Is Consistency.

Pavlov consistently offered food to the dogs every time he rang the bell. Every time.

### Key Number Two Is Frequency

He didn't do a weekend blitz of feeding and bell ringing; he did it week-in and week-out for many weeks and months.

### Key Number Three Is Anchoring

When you are imbedding an associative memory, you must have a recall cue. In Pavlov's case, the recall cue is the bell. The bell had better be tied to something already in the mind of the customer. In Pavlov's case, the bell became linked to the dog's love for meat.

**What if Pavlov decided to brand the dogs with flea collars?**

Every morning he would place a very nice flea collar on the dog, tell the dog how good the flea collar is and ring a bell. After a few days, there would be a bent bell and teeth marks on certain parts of Pavlov's anatomy.

Is the repetitive part of your ads, your jingle or slogan tied to an anchor that is already in the heart of your customer?

Or… maybe you enjoy irritating people with your ads.

## Chapter 21

## BRANDING RELATIONAL CUSTOMERS

There are two different types of customers and you are both of them. When you buy some products and services you are relational in the purchase. When we buy other products or services you are transactional in the purchase.

The **relational customer** is thinking long-term. They consider today's transaction to be one in a series of many. They look to you as a resource for their needs. They do not enjoy comparison shopping or negotiating. Their only fear is making the wrong choice. The Relational customer hopes to find an expert they can trust. They consider their time spent shopping as part of the purchase price. They are most likely to become a repeat customer.

The **transactional customer** is thinking short term. They care only about today's transaction. They actually enjoy the process of shopping and the negotiating. The biggest fear they have is paying more than they had to pay. Transactional customers are willing to spend time investigating and researching products and services. They consider themselves to be the expert. You'll recognize them because they are the ones carrying a copy of *Consumers Report* and the ads of your competitors. Most of all, every transaction hinges on price.

I am transactional when it comes to buying a car and relational when it comes to buying a computer.

When I buy a car, I do the research ahead of time and try to know more about the car than the salesman I am talking with. All car dealers look the same to me; they all have basically the same car selling system. You know what I mean, the sales person marches back and forth between you and his manager at trying to work you the best deal he or she possibly can. Gag me!

When it's time for me to buy anything PC computer related, I go to CompUSA and talk to Riley or I go to BDS Computers and talk to the owner Bob. Why? Because I want to make the right decision and I trust these guys to steer me in the right direction. I know I can call one of these guys and get their opinion and good advice anytime. Whatever the price is, that's what I pay, no hype, no haggling. When I come across someone who needs a car, I really don't know where to send him or her. When I run across someone who has a computer need, even if it's someone I just met in a crowded restaurant, I become a walking, talking billboard for Riley at CompUSA and Bob at BDS Computers.

Again, the customer can be a relational shopper in one product category and a transactional shopper in another.

How does all of this apply to radio advertising?

Who do you think is a better candidate to advertise to, the transactional shopper or the relational shopper? The transactional shopper is the one on the hunt for your sale. The only way they will purchase your product is if it is marked down to the bone. I believe you call that a shrinking profit margin. The relational customer is looking for the right choice. If you have the right choice, they will pay whatever price you are asking.

**Tell them your entire story and their story over time!**

The best way to use radio to reach relational customers is to develop a long-long term advertising strategy. Pretend you are going to read a book to thousands of people over time. Your book contains hundreds of sixty-second chapters. You are going to tell the same audience your story and that of your business over time. You will tell them specific, factual stories they understand and can relate to. You are going to tell the listener their story and why they need you. You will make them laugh and cry. Your journey will be part of their journey. **Your goal is to slowly plant seeds of knowledge about you and your products and services over time.**

**THEN, WHEN THEY NEED YOU, THEY WILL THINK OF YOU FIRST AND FEEL BEST ABOUT YOU AND THEY WILL CALL YOU.**

## Chapter 22
## THE MARKETING BOAT

**You can** buy word of mouth, but it won't be effective…

…if you don't sound trustworthy.

…if your commercials sound like commercials.

…if you are not consistently talking to the same audience.

…If you use "ad-Speak"

**and if you have holes in your marketing boat!!!**

**The Marketing Bridge**

Business consultant Chuck Mefford of Lighthouse Communications (see www.brandsformation.com) teaches an excellent study on "the marketing bridge." The marketing bridge includes everything that links the customer to the sale and everything that separates the customer from the sale. Mefford breaks down the marketing bridge into five basic areas.

First is your **Competitiveness.** How does your business compare with your competitors? Do your customers walk away satisfied? What competitive advantage is your business offering in the marketplace?

The second step of the bridge is **Merchandising**. Do you have nice curb appeal? Would someone want to stop simply by driving by? Is your location clean inside and out? Do you feel "invited in" when you walk across the threshold of the main entrance? How often are your displays rotated and do you have an annual floor game plan? Are your stores hours convenient to your customers or convenient to the storeowner? What about your signage? Can you spot your store sign easily from ¼ mile away? Does your sign reflect your image or the image of your sign maker? In a recent study, well lit merchandise sold 3-to-1 over poorly lit merchandise in the same store. How is your lighting? Your price tags must be easy to find and if you're having a sale, even easier to find. Are your products season appropriate, can I buy swimming suits in the summer and snow blowers in the winter? Are your aisles wide enough to get through? Do you have a common-sense and relevant floor plan?     Is the coffee next to the doughnuts at one end of the store and at the other end do you have the oil and the washer-fluid?  Do you have a window presentation?  Is it appealing?

The third step in the marketing bridge is **Personal Selling Skills**.  Is there a relatively quick greeting? Is your staff cheerful and sincere?  Is your staff trained to focus on solving customer needs?  How is your staff's appearance?  Is there a consistency in their dress code? Is it obvious who is an employee and who is not? Does your sales staff use personal recommendations after using the products themselves? Are they able to paint a picture of how your product or service should be used for best results?  Does your staff make accessory suggestions that actually make sense?

The fourth step in the marketing bridge is the **Customer's Perspective.** Does your business represent quality product lines?  Are you getting good word-of-mouth from your current customers?  Do you give back to the community? Do you have a simple return policy? Do you always do what you say you will do?  Do you take cash, checks, the four main credit cards, are there credit options and is there an ATM on site?  Are your bathrooms as clean as they can possibly be? How many potential customers have you on one of the top three rungs of the positioning ladder?

The fifth step of the marketing bridge is **Advertising**. Are you branding or are you advertising an event?  Is your message clear?  Are you getting enough frequency? Are you advertising 52 weeks a year and getting enough consistency? Is your staff always aware of your promotions?  Are you offering the public something only you can offer in your market?

**Chapter 23**

**THE MARKETING BOAT ILLUSTRATION**

If you consider your business a boat, you can row it yourself. If your boat has holes in it or if parts of your marketing bridge are missing, you are going to sink. If you strap on the motor of advertising without patching the holes, you'll go down faster. Advertising only speeds up to what's going to happen anyway. If you're good at what you do, you will grow faster. If you suck like a Hoover, you will sink with amazing speed!

This next illustration has proven to be a great way for me to help my clients understand the aspects of the Marketing Bridge. The Marketing Bridge is a series of steps between you and your potential customer. Some things need to be built up and some need to be torn down in order for people to become your customer. One day in a dialog with a client, I said your business is like a boat that you can row by yourself or your can strap the engine of advertising to it and make sales happen faster. In fact that is what advertising does. It speeds up what is going to happen anyway. If you are good at what you do, you will go up faster. If you are bad at what you do, you will go down faster. That evening I went home and ended up with the following illustration...

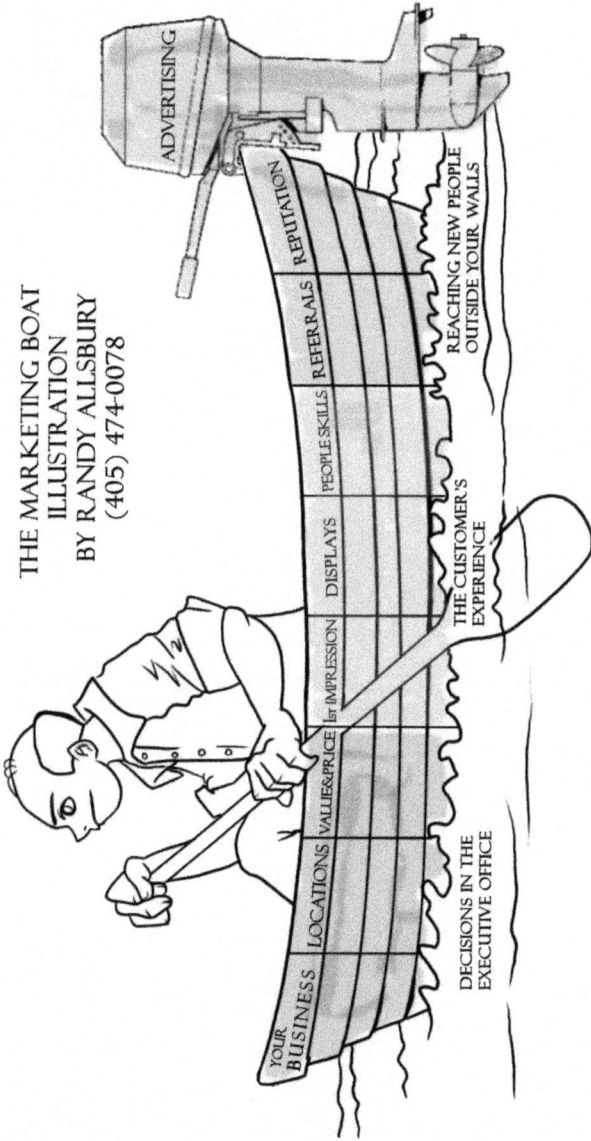

THE MARKETING BOAT
ILLUSTRATION
BY RANDY ALLSBURY
(405) 474-0078

ADVERTISING

YOUR BUSINESS | LOCATIONS | VALUE&PRICE | 1st IMPRESSION | DISPLAYS | PEOPLE SKILLS | REFERRALS | REPUTATION

DECISIONS IN THE EXECUTIVE OFFICE

THE CUSTOMER'S EXPERIENCE

REACHING NEW PEOPLE OUTSIDE YOUR WALLS

## Chapter 24

## A DOZEN ADVERTISING PRINCIPLES

**"Methods are many, principles are few. Methods always change, principles never do!"**

1. People don't hate advertising, **they hate stupid commercials that don't involve them.**

2. **If a commercial sounds or looks like a commercial, it's a bad commercial.**

3. **Speak to individuals**, in the language of individuals, about what matters to individuals.

4. Always do long-term campaigns with a series of ads that are **like chapters of a book. The book is your story and that of the reader or listener.**

5. **Rely on consistent, frequent INTRUSIVE media.** TV, radio and billboards are INTRUSIVE. The other side of that coin is PASSIVE media. PASSIVE media

requires action on the part of the consumer.
INTRUSIVE media only requires them to be present to
hear or easily read.

6. YES YOU CAN AFFORD TV, RADIO OR
BILLBOARDS!!! **You just can't afford to reach your
entire city.** One client built her law firm with two
billboards that cost $250.00 a month each. Over the past
few years she has gone from renting a little office for
$500.00 a month to owning her own law office building
. (She had a message that mattered!)

7. **You have to be competent, friendly and real for
people to like you.** "All things being equal, people want
to do business with people they like. All things not
being equal, people still want to do business with people
they like!"

8. Raise your value, don't lower your price. What is
value? It is the difference between the anticipated cost of
the consumer and the actual cost when they get the bill.
If you have a junky-cheap looking place of business,
people will assume your prices are low. If you have a
very nice, high-end place of business, people will

assume your prices are high. **VALUE IS THE DIFFERENCE BETWEEN THE ANTICIPATED COST AND THE ACTUAL COST. (If your actual cost is lower.)**

9. **Expensive rent is cheap advertising.** Generally, it costs more to be where people are. Generally, it costs less to be in a warehouse district on the edge of town.

10. Know the Marketing Boat. Make sure your business boat doesn't have holes in it! See illustration.

11. Be where people are and **have a big sign that says what you do!** You would be amazed how many business owners have a great location and a sign that says "Johnson Enterprises" out front. What the heck is "Johnson Enterprises"?

12. **"We judge others by their actions. We judge ourselves by our intentions."** You are inside your bottle and can't read your own label. Ask someone outside of your bottle to help you see yourself as your customers actually see you.

**Number 12 is the best thing I can give my clients.** The ability to see you like the world sees you. Many times what is most obvious to the rest of the world is resting quietly in the blind spot of the business owner.

It takes courage to face the truth. It takes humility to allow someone else to point out your blind spots.

DO YOU HAVE COURAGE?